SELECTED

Selected Poems

KIRKPATRICK DOBIE

PETERLOO POETS

First published in 1992
by Peterloo Poets
2 Kelly Gardens, Calstock, Cornwall PL18 9SA, U.K.

© 1992 by Kirkpatrick Dobie

All rights reserved. No part of this publication may be reproduced, stored in a retrieval system, or transmitted, in any form or by any means, electronic, mechanical, photocopying, recording or otherwise without the prior permission in writing of the publisher.

A catalogue record for this book is available from the British Library

ISBN 1-871471-36-2

Printed in Great Britain by
Latimer Trend & Company Ltd, Plymouth

Supported by
Cornwall
County Council

**INVESTMENT
SOUTH WEST ARTS**

For Ann Karkalas

Contents

page
- 9 Dumfries
- 10 Girl at a Close
- 11 My Father
- 12 Uncle John
- 13 Sidney
- 14 The Blaishie
- 15 The Grahams
- 16 John Jackson
- 18 Stephenson Statue Outside the Public Library
- 19 Pictures
- 20 Preface to a Book of Poems About Dogs
- 22 Old Woman Lost
- 23 Mabie Woods
- 24 Summerfield
- 25 Curriestanes
- 26 Divinity 1
- 28 Loreburn Street
- 30 Mrs Cleeberg
- 31 Church on Weekdays
- 32 On the Eve
- 34 Before the Cenotaph
- 36 Lt. Col. Knowles
- 37 Kangaroo
- 38 Aberfan
- 40 Gasometer
- 43 Pittenweem
- 49 King Claudius
- 51 Mary Wollstonecraft
- 52 Samuel Dyer
- 54 Easter and After
- 56 Philip Larkin
- 57 Ca Ira!
- 61 Snow in Lent
- 62 Last Words

Dumfries

Dumfries
my comfortable conforming town
lies on a firth. The sea
from time to time encroaches,
so with me.
'Hell is a city very like Seville'
the poet says,
and might have added that they never knew
who only knew Seville
and slept in peace
as in Dumfries.

So
keepsakes, snapshots, echoes —
what you will,
figures of speech —
stand bulwarks against time, buoys
to mark love and hope.
I hold them steady in my mind
against demise
of that content
that makes Dumfries
Dumfries.

Girl at a Close

My mother was a Friars Vennel girl.
I picture her, a child in frilly drawers
emerging from this gap beside the shop
a shade uncertain. Emerging, but inclined to stop.

Shy, pulling at her cotton pinafore —
in those days little girls were always shy,
and being sole survivor of so many,
she'd reason. I click the camera on anxiety.

Next scene the same: the closemouth. Now she stands
Young Woman with Collie Dog—a Border type—
hat wide-brimmed, cherry-trimmed, lace parasol.
Perfect! The dog the same. I think he was called Noble . . .

Hold this! It's like a *Waiting in the Wings*.
Uncertain still, yet knowing her appeal,
I hold her, tremulous in her waitingness.
Old Man with Camera full of protectiveness.

My Father

My father was a man for stopping horses.
To screams and yells
preceded by a rattling rising roar
the beast appeared,
head reared,
eye rolling black-blobbed swum in white,
battering the cobbles with a bounding cart,
frenzied to freeze the heart.

But at the sight my father's spirit rose
and as the echoes rang
he ran and sprang
high at the rampant head
and bore it down;
with all of fourteen stone
muscle and bone,
hung! and hung on!

I've never visited his grave.
I couldn't stand and moralise
or seem to take his size.
What I remember doesn't lie
in any cemetery.
I have his stick
rough-handled, thick,
and now in my own wintry weather
stumble or slip
I feel his grip.

Uncle John

John was the joker of the pack.
One of his jokes had been to brand his brother.
They shared a bed to which my uncle Tom
early repaired and largely occupied.
John, coming home from nightshift, tired of this
and one night puffed upon his pipe
until the metal top was red.
He then applied it to his brother's bum.
Tom, though disturbed, slept on.
(He was a heavy sleeper.) 'D'ye see ocht there?'
he asked next morning, tugging at his shirt.
'Naething by ordinar', John prevaricated.
It was a family joke often repeated.

Another joke followed a heart-attack;
my father, asking how he was,
being invited to throw down a match.
Picking it up, 'Ah'm better', he pronounced.
'Ah was telt onything like that 'ud kill me.
But, as ye see, it hisnae.'

I hardly knew him but recall
last days at Moniaive, a sleepy land-locked place,
and something said about a bull
that bellowed at unseasonable hours.
It was for slaughter and had seemed to cry—
'Sentenced to death! Sentenced to death!'
Now, not his jokes, but sleepless in the night
the sick man listening, waiting for the light,
is what I most remember.

Sidney

I had always thought I should see him,
that one day he'd appear at the door
but now no more

can I entertain such a notion
or think we will talk about things past
seated at last

in my small tucked-away back office
in Loreburn Street near Dobie's Wynd.
It's in my mind

I'd have found means to mention it—
'Dobie's'. But that's all done and over
now, forever.

I could have seen him anytime I'd
cared to take the car a dozen miles
and cross two stiles.

Is it I thought we were immortal?
No. Rather so much of me he was
and so, because

he was so near, it made postponement
like the exigency of verse, a groove
preventing love.

*The Blaishie**

'These people never knew Roy Austin.'
—Elderly man leaving St Michael's High Cemetery.

Attending Roy Austin's funeral.
It's happening at the High
where the intersection of roads makes a mural,
a Lowry-like setting of mourners, with an odd car speeding
    by.

Umbrellas confer at the graveside,
the grave itself almost hid
by grave men huddled as if they had something to hide.
All old, and Roy too must be old, under that coffin lid.

Hard to think it, remembering The Blaishie.
What I remember is joy.
The minister's word but a different species.
Wild! Wild as young blood—or a thought that he's risen to
    scatter 'em!
—Roy!

* A hamlet of doubtful reputation.

The Grahams

The Grahams came before John Jackson
and stayed to be an object lesson,
running the *Coach & Horses* till it crashed
and their effects and ineffectualness became
a warrant sale
upon the pavement at the front street door.

I knew this only as excitement, now recalled
as something else;
the barmaid-wife, big-bosomed blowsy,
snatching from out the heart of loss, a crystal boy
(it had held whisky) smuggling it in my jersey as she kissed.
'A gift' she says, 'for you. A keepsake.'

I didn't keep her keepsake long.
It was too frail. Yet in some sense
it seems it still survives and makes me think
nothing perhaps is ever lost, and that
is quite a thought.

Not necessarily for comfort.

John Jackson

I am not one for visiting the sick.
I see it too much as intrusion. Almost
a taking of advantage, but
at the moment when I pressed his hand
I saw him not as sick but savage,
riding a one-time customer and friend,
beating the traitor's backside like a drum,
his carpet slipper a baton
to grunts and roars, and at each stroke
the dust flew up to meet the golden shaft
streamed from the fanlight of the front street-door.
What it was all about, I did not (do not) know.
It could be anything and it was thirty years ago.

'My mother sent me here', I'd started off . . .
(He had been downstair-tenant of my mother
so there was obligation. Also,
being timid, I admired assertion,
and, thinking of it now, remembering
the brazed brown bowler tilted to one side,
the morning paper holstered like a gun—
it was John Bull—
and realising all the rage
of such a man in such an occupation—
he was a fishing-tackle maker—
the faky nature of the work,
the interruptions and exasperations,
the small rewards, and I suspect,
the loneliness, I still admire—and grieve,
though at the time I only longed to leave).

'I'll hope to see you better.' This was said
as I retired. 'No! No! Ye'll no dae that!'
And then, collecting all his failing powers,
he cried out in a loud hoarse voice: 'Onywey!
Ah hope tae see that bugger Maxwell-Imrie
away afore me!'

Appalling, and I was appalled, and yet,
had Keats not said a quarrel in the streets
though hateful, was in some respects sublime?
I thought that true, and faithfulness to one's own nature
    must
count something, somehow, somewhere,
as minus multiplied by minus makes a plus.

Stephenson Statue Outside the Public Library

Meticulous, intent,
he kneels oblivious
to weather and neglect.
The little engine in his hands
remains unbroken yet.

Delicate, dedicate,
I think and it comes back,
his contribution—steam!
'That first fit locomotive'—his!
That forward step his dream.

Who now, worse than forgot,
an effigy consigned
to squalor and defeat,
stares at the age he ushered in,
itself half obsolete.

And yet, perhaps because
so oddly brought to mind
I trace on wakeful nights
dark fields to an abandoned track
and look for moving lights.

Pictures

We went on Saturdays when we could raise the pence,
saw *Exploits of Elaine*
in a green rain
and Mary Pickford rescued from the train.
Fairbanks and Fu Man Chu
we knew
better than kin.
They were more true.

But truer, vivider,
though screened at Sunday School,
was *Abram's Sacrifice*.
The Upper Hall in Irish Street remains,
the wooden stair
is there,
trod now by fewer.
(It's said the fabric's insecure.)
Oh! for a Faith that Will not Shrink!
we sang, but now I think
this too, unsure.

Anyhow, there was Isaac trussed
and bearded Abram brandishing the knife
as large as life.
Love, this was love,
it was explained
but what remained
and is remembered
is the knife.

Preface (to a book of poems about dogs)

I remember Mackie Sanderson
talking of dogs and field-trials
tell how at Saxmundham
he stayed overnight
with handlers and owners—
all of them in,
all, after the second day,
still with a chance to win.

They'd sat round the fire
and thoughts turned to life
as often they do
after hours in the open,
a meal and a drink,
life and dogs going together.
To them the same thing I should think.

Anyhow, somebody told how on Sundays
he'd get up at six
and still in pyjamas
pull socks on and gum-boots
and wrapped in a mackintosh
let out the dogs
to the fields and the fallow
the hedgerows and sough

the whole pack of them—Labradors—
yelping and squabbling
and he striding on
head down to the wind
or up to the sun.
The wide world of it
glistering!
all the two miles to the station.

Then home. Back the same way,
but different.
For it's never the same.
Back to beer and grilled bacon
and then into bed
with the Sunday papers
and the dogs fed.

It was accepted by everyone present,
said Mackie,
that this was supreme for the human condition.
Thinking of poetry I couldn't agree
but I know what he meant
for I see

At odd moments increasingly often
that man on his way to a low Lowland skyline,
the dogs nosing and circling,
running out wide and returning,
raising perhaps a rabbit or plover
and the man—the moving centre of it—
with a snipe or a hawk going over.

It's forty five years and an age, since my brother
was killed—early too—on a similar morning
on the railway near Marchhill, not far from the town,
the bitch ambling the metals
deaf to her danger, confused somehow,
flattening herself, refusing to budge,
and he, reaching out to her, struck on the brow.

Not the worst way to die, and not even, I think,
a life thrown away.
We thought of the bitch when we thought of my brother.
Not to sift or equate, or to separate,
for in one sense the balance was trim:
we knew without wording it, she being dog,
would have done it for him.

So the verses that follow
are not so much sad, but more celebration
of dogs who played dead-dog
till the game turned to earnest
as it does; yet remembered by us
not sad, never sad,
but for ever as innocent, loving and joyous.

Old Woman Lost

So slow my wits
I'm halfway to the stair
calling his name
who isn't there.

Into the dark
he went, and what he heard—
a cry perhaps,
perhaps a bird—

who knows? I know
I live the epilogue
like a lost dog.

Mabie Woods

I take the dog to Mabie Woods.
She is a bitch and furtive, shy,
a collie-cross. They come that way—
unsettled, with a leery eye.

But in the woods she shows no fear.
She bounces on from tree to tree.
Head down and haunches high she goes.
I take a pleasure in her glee.

The woods are quiet. Off the road
you cannot hear a passing car,
and underneath their twining roof
you never think how still they are.

Until you mark some little sound:
the snap of twig, the cry of bird,
and feel the touch upon the web
that yet does nothing to disturb.

I bring my troubles to the woods
and troubles that are more than mine:
the senseless Irish thuggery,
the butchery in Palestine.

And somehow, there they die away,
and like the bitch's are forgot.
Mine, in my senses' atrophy,
hers, in her senses' riot.

Summerfield

Tall poppies grow beside the stile,
some partly hidden by the hedge,
and some that brush the upper rail
are rooted at the very edge.

In June of every year they come
red-orange-tipped and irised-brown.
They sway towards you as you pass
and touch your hand as you step down.

Great gangling girls, they never learn
how much of men is purely brute,
so every year they come again
and some are trampled underfoot.

Curriestanes

Nature to me was never all in all.
I like it best when bare;
not in deep clefts or lanes
of cherry-ripe montage
and blossom camouflage,
but where the hawthorn hedge
cut back, makes rough the edge,
as here at Curriestanes.

For the same reason otherwise expressed
I choose to take the air
not on the mountain tops
where rain is hail or snow
and every gust a blow,
but as a passer-by
with an indifferent eye
and on the lower slopes.

The images *I* make are permanent things.
They represent the facts,
but always with them twinned
are shapes, not of delight,
but such as steal at night
from caves and crevasses
of dim uneasiness
to sniff and sift the wind.

Half town, half country, that is best. To stand
where the first stars appear
and car-lights light the clouds,
and know, if not to see,
at hand the vertebrae:
those ancient mottled stones,
the sunken road's bare bones,
pock-marked, peep from their shrouds.

Divinity 1

I saw the Nile in Nith the other night,
its reeds and mud against a western sky,
all mild and mellow in an amber light
as I looked down the Solway estuary.
But soon enough came clouds of flitting bats
and byre-sick bellowings from Cargen Flatts.

Up from the river by the old Kirkgate
the bridge is mellow too in reds and greens,
its cobbles smoothed each day from six to eight
are art assiduous as the fellaheens'.
So delicate, so pale, these sculptured stones,
under the moon a pyramid of bones.

Cockburn is buried by St Michael's door.
In deep B-flat the bell above him beats,
but stirs no echo on Caerlaverock shore
except the wind in Kelton's wynds repeats.
And then the wind becomes his muezzin
proclaiming an apostasy no sin.

Jehovah or Osiris, what's the odds?
I see the Nile in Nith, it needs no gown.
It nothing adds to name the name of gods
or put a benediction on the town.
To add degree is to do something dead.
God is a very common thing—like bread.

There's loss in ordination. It's a bar
against uncovenanted gamin grace,
thicker than that through which shines Sirius' star
for forty fathoms on the Pharoah's face.
The eager anxious boy to Moses grown
turns from the burning bush to slabs of stone.

I throw a net of words and keep no score
and in the vacant places of my art—
between the lines as through an open door—
comes sometimes something where I have no part.
Not anything I know of sound or sight
or re-creation in a golden light.

But when it comes, it comes with gentlest guile,
or hammer-hard as on a finger nail.
Or as, 'twixt worshippers, quick down the aisle
some glancing girl goes meek as Abigail.
Or high across the estuary at night
like the right words, wild geese in frosty flight.

Loreburn Street

Of many others, Mackie Sanderson is one,
Hitler and Mussolini were to him
'The Beaconlights of Anti-Christ',
Baldwin, 'A meretricious mandragora'.
I could go on, but what to say
of Roberts, Copeland, Hannon (flint-faced, kind),
rugged Joe Scott, Tom Bell and Gallemore,
Laurie and Hutchison,
Clark, Birrel, Shiel, Bob Symonds and McCall,
Coleman and Milligan, John Paul?

Except
that horses, dogs, game and game-prospects were
their life who came about our store
and Saturday nights sat round the fire,
parcels at feet.
So solid, stolid, permanent they seemed
rockfast forever, but are gone
no more than smoke that drifted from their pipes,
thoughts of an ageing man.

*

My limitation was to see them as a group,
a post-war generation. World War One,
so solemnised and cenotaphed,
had not begun to burst its cerements.
It therefore came as something of a shock
to learn that Jake had been a sniper.
He was too ordinary. At thirty-nine
too boyish-gauche, and, as it seemed,
too innocent.
In the end I had to ask—and ask, until
turning away his head—
'My God! Ye couldnae miss!' was what he said.

I wished that I had held my tongue,
and somehow later, counting out the cash,
or putting books away, there came to mind
what I had seen one night on Pathé News—
a harpooned turtle dragged up from the deep,
clawing the gunwale, poised, all blood,
its prehistoric face
staring expressionless upon the human race.

Mrs Cleeberg

When I hear of compassion—especially from politicians—
it makes me feel sick.
The word 'dignity' too, makes me squeamish
and even 'equality' sounds to my ear like the start of
a confidence trick.

I date all this to nineteen fourteen and old Mrs Cleeberg
in her long nightgown
fleeing from patriots—she was German-born—
tearing her legs to bits on barbed wire in fields at the Stoop
as she stumbled on.

At least, we had the grace to keep quiet about it, this—first
of our casualties.
In fact, it was seldom, if ever, discussed,
lost in accounts of rape, ruin, destruction and death—
Hun-atrocities!

Church on Weekdays

This church is hollow.
Footsteps explode, reverberate,
echo,
echoing nothing.
It is nothing in high arches.

But once at a wedding
an old auctioneer
told dirty stories
then,
as if not changing the subject,
spoke of love
and the place—
a licensed hotel—
became altered.

Again, at a station
near Pondicherry,
the train stopped for natives
to see the Mahatma—
thousands and thousands
milling and shouting
till he appeared and you heard him
plainly,
high and thin like a child:

> Blessed were the poor in spirit,
> the meek,
> the peacemakers and the merciful,
> and the pure in heart
> for they would see God.

It came as a shock for I had expected Urdu,
not something in English that I had heard often.
A bony old urchin, he rises to mind,
and the train and the crowd,
and the engine hissing in the heat.

On the Eve

(Calcutta 1947. From *Tides of Fortune*, Macmillan.)

Under the shade of the Banyan tree
Mr Macmillan sat with Wyndham,
guest of honour doing the honours
at a party by Mr Biswas,
friend and colleague of Mr Brindle,
sole editor of *Nature*,
a sound Macmillan publication.

Mr Macmillan thought it funny—
'politics apart'—how pleased they were,
how gratified by minor favour.
Gravely they spoke of Education,
Art, Anthropology, Religion,
avoiding though, Amritsar,
though naturally they knew about it.

So, on the terrace amiably,
making uplifting conversation:
Mr Macmillan, Mr Wyndham.
Meanwhile there floated past in relays
numerous decomposing bodies
harried by flocks of vultures
also on business, ready for risk.

The vulture, Macmillan knew quite well,
is unaquatic; to seize the eyes—
its prize—it dives, brakes, stalls and grabs the face.
The corpse, as animated, sidles,
rolls, bobs, evades, and part submerges;
follows a floundering take-off
then that persistent seige returning.

Macmillan saw it all, and Wyndham
also remarked, but perfect manners
comment forbade. Instead, the talk
turned to the future, on which their hosts
were of good hope though inexplicit.
The country would unite—Yes!
Freedom, democracy—Yes! Oh yes!

Before the Cenotaph

I dreamed about the Cenotaph last night.
    I was near the library
in Catherine Street, and stood there in half-light
    almost as if I'd lost a memory.

Yet it was more a carry-forward—
    this twilight shadowness I mean—
not to be thought as something untoward
    but an extension of the normal scene:

this modern world of which we are a part
    its altered countryside,
its architecture hideous as a wart,
    its sum, vulgarity diversified.

All this I saw—or knew—the broken roads,
    the sullen public service,
streets cumbered up with cars as squat as toads,
    I saw them as the civic body-lice.

I thought of New-crop Carse of Stirling Hay
    green-cut and tightly pressed,
sweet-smelling stems now turned out any way,
    the stale stack bottoms baled in with the rest.

And there were small existences pent up:
    sad animals, sick tortoises,
the frog, the newt, the wide-eyed frightened pup,
    the factory-farm's condoned atrocities.

And I remembered things far-fetched in grief:
    Southey's precocious infant son,
gone like a brilliant out-of-autumn leaf
    before its summer season had begun;

and even further-fetched, of the Graf Speé
    and Landorf's suicide,
things wholly unconnected you might say
    except in each an innocence had died.

Here, in this ancient town, the slights
    of mindless social scorn,
and talk of dignity and human rights
    from those who kill the unborn.

Such was the scene: cant and brutality,
    religion lost to sense.
A Church of Scotland like the IRA,
    faithless to God, its faith in violence.

No mist in that! But then I caught my breath,
    Tobruk and Singapore
I saw, and saw it as the final death
    that nothing would be thought worth fighting for.

And while these wraiths whirled in my mind like chaff
    it seemed at last I stood
in broad daylight before the Cenotaph
    and saw that every name on it ran blood.

Lt. Col. Knowles

Obit 1987

In nineteen twenty two in Srinagar
he set out with a friend to kill a bear.
Nothing vindictive. Any bear would do.

A bear was found and speedily despatched.
It tumbled headlong down a steep ravine
whence, having first restrained the Shirikas—
for he was nothing if not well-disposed—
the Colonel followed. Presently,
with a loud 'Woof!' the creature reappeared
'heading towards him, this time on all fours.'

What happened next remains unclear.
It seems the pathway broke, the Colonel fell,
the bear advanced, then everything went black.
When he revived it was to tears
rained down upon him by the Shirikas.
The bear was dead.

All this was in *The Daily Telegraph*
with details of a subsequent career.
Promotions, decorations,
busy retirement during which he served
in Suffolk as a County Councillor.

Bears do not have obituaries
but all the same
some mention of an unprovoked attack
and an unequal fight bravely resumed
might have been made and—how I hardly know—
presented somehow as a sort of test.
Not of the sort to do with fame or glory,
still less to make an after-dinner story,
but of civilisation.

Kangaroo

In Australasia the kangaroo
is killed for dog meat. This to expose,
Allsop, a TV personage, sets out
and with the monetary side arranged,
accompanies a hunter to the bush
and shoots him as he shoots the kangaroo.

Appropriately
the work is done in half-light—dusk or dawn.
Caught in reflector-glare the kangaroo
dies, and is skinned with instant expertise:
head, feet, and tail slashed off, the carcass trimmed,
the guts and those lopped members left behind
for ants and other little pensioners;
the small amount of blood drains in the sand
and very soon, had Allsop not been there
the truth, in some respects, had been unknown,
before and after being much the same.

The BBC has numerous officials
whose mission is continuously to serve,
and if they cannot find the thing they seek
they demonstrate to prove that it exists.
This being so, one often is in doubt
just how to take their presentations.
Here, the effect owed nothing to design:
an unsuspecting hunter's bald account
of an ungainly panic-stricken creature
scrambling to hide its life behind a tree
but peeping round the bole against the light
a sitting target, like himself—and us.

Aberfan

In mining Wales at Aberfan
across the fields the mountain ran
and choked the little children where
they stood in rows at morning prayer.

Before the parents knew their dead
they knew what some pronouncer said
and how he felt and how he looked
and fathers saw themselves rebuked
that such a broken busy man
should bear the grief of Aberfan.
But others were as quick as he
to show how sorry they could be,
for sorrow must compete no less
than any other business.
Grave, gracious, condescending, quick,
candid, confiding, every trick!
They ran where each sensation led,
did it like Marlborough—'for bread'.
The knowing boys who only know
life as a story, death a show.

> And shows and shams and Abbadon
> were all they had at Aberfan,
> and money poured in like a flood
> to make a deeper sea of mud.

Christ! was there nobody to shame them?
Reproach and drive them out and blame them?
With everything that there belongs—
a tongue to scourge! A whip with thongs!
Nothing! The Church saw nothing wrong.
They only wanted to belong.
Their only horror was the fate
of seeming to be out of date.
Not love, but what they called compassion
they followed, for it was the fashion.

But better far for Aberfan
had all the loving hearts withdrawn
and held their tongues and dried their eyes
and stayed at home divinely wise,
leaving the village to the fact,
the brute unmitigated act,
awe-ful, obscure, but wholly kin
to that bleak world they wandered in.
The silence of the empty street,
the grimy grass beneath their feet,
the moving moon in a dark sky
had been their kinder company.

    But tragic, tragic, Aberfan,
    where all around the show-men ran
    and showed the people how they bled
    and left them deader than their dead.

Gasometer

'You can't make a poem about a gasometer.'—Old saying.

When I left Hull
in '42
my mind was dull
and empty too.

In foreign lands
I learnt a lot
in desert sands
a polyglot.

The grimy streets
the smoky skies
the policeman's beats
of Paradise

I left behind
or so I thought.
I mucked my mind
of all the lot.

When back again
to Hull I came,
Hull in the rain,
Hull just the same,

by forty five
battered a bit
but still as I've
remembered it.

The soggy night
wet as a clam
stuck to me tight.
I took a tram.

God! Such a chase
and such a fright!
The bloody place
was flattened quite!

From Boxer's Rise
the Gerry's doin'
all Paradise
a scattered ruin.

(By roof and gable
rain laments
indecipherable
tenements.

Like a sick face
the moon appears,
a ruff of lace
about her ears.)

That gleam's the sea—
There's the North Dock—
Here's Trinity . . .
the Steeple clock . . .

That hoarding there
the Palace Theatre . . .
An' there—but where—
the Gasometer?

I turned about.
I felt no pain.
The moon passed out
in rain again.

Identity's
a compromise.
It's what you see
and recognise.

Take that away
and what you knew
is vacancy
and so are you.

So null and dull
and half-alive
I went from Hull
in forty-five.

Pittenweem

To my imagination comes the place;
now, as I hear her loud harsh peacock cry,
I see the broken paths and touch the trace
of lichen on the sullen statuary.
I take the teacup and I feel the breath
of that conformity subscribed to death.

This is a moment when the active heart
drum-major prompt, beating the thick blood on,
loses self-confidence and would depart
its unconsidered labour and be gone.
When thought that thought itself a special birth
thinks of its long affinity with earth.

This earth! This obstinate veracity.
Persistent as desire, as dull as sleep.
It is our meaning and the means whereby
we live and have our being, and we creep
slow to an understanding of defeat:
life is a drunk man in a silent street.

For I have seen the parties, dances, dinners,
like the recurrence of the equinox
turn boisterous youth to less assertive sinners,
making their gaiety a paradox.
And marked the score as each remembered face
was absent from the not-less-festive place.

I think of Fletcher when his boy was dead
and buried two or three days—perhaps a week.
He couldn't get the child out of his head
but though in every way as tough as teak,
went out one night in a wild make-believe
and spread a coat over the soaking grave.

Pathetic that. Though if we live again
it must be in the flesh and nothing less,
to know with nerves and apprehend in pain,
not any hocus-pocus ghostliness—
the lipless whisper in the darkened room,
the shadeless shadow in the deeper gloom.

Yet to think this is surely to think thought
to be no more oneself than foot or hand
and raises echoes of old battles fought,
a tedious command and countermand
of things disputive to the very brink
where flesh and Fletcher in each other sink—

and merge and fuse, enfold or intertwine
so to become a kind of horse and cart,
a doubleton produced without design,
the issue of an uncontriving art.
A predetermined mix of random motes
where consciousness like a vague aura floats?

*

Begin again, and this time stand aside
to slip the quick conveyor-belt of being;
observing it, do I remain as tied?
Is this self-conscious verse not free agreeing?
Then why not Paul's enquiring spirit's breath
struggling within the body of its death?

The movement of the mind like tracks of birds
across these winnowed sands, now lucent, bare,
resembling too, in transience, my words,
may, from some other, uncorrupted sphere,
be native to a kingdom whose degree
is unimaginable liberty.

May be. And maybe only very nice.
Not true at all, or just a truth of choice.
The word, employed not in the sense 'precise',
but rather as one listens to one's voice
conning the admass, doing it so well
that one is almost half-convinced oneself.

Yet, take the truth to be we have freewill—
what the unthinking think themselves to be—
what difference does it make? I sit here still
and choice itself remains the mystery.
Freewill, it seems, is such a strong delusion
it couldn't be more true if no illusion.

*

Autumnal Kodaks of my early days!
Assurance of a light no longer seen,
of one who never knew a madding maze
or saw it only as a pure serene.
Within the little Lethe of my mind
he rises, happiest of all mankind—

that best philosopher, the butcher loon
I knew in youth, who scamped his work and fled
each golden glorious idle afternoon
to the green meadows by the watershed.
And didn't even fish, but in the shade
reclined, and sent small boys for lemonade.

So near, so clear, and yet how long ago
the apprentice-killer fell beneath the steel
but 'Dulce et decorum est'—the plaque says so,
though with a certain irony, I feel.
Not sweet or fitting is a bloody skewer
and 'Died reluctantly' would have been truer.

*

The good die young but not the coarser thing
sib to the dirt, the penetrable clay,
rouge on the butcher bird's flirtatious wing,
an iridescence on the bone's decay.
Goading the strong and trampling down the weak,
what in the name of loving does it seek?

Not peace at least, for all its ways are war
and in the Amazonian jungle striped and lean
the fighting cats not more malignant are
than in the L-shaped rooms of Pittenweem.
Where, over teacups homo sapiens bends
whetting her tongue upon the absent friends.

I see its shape as civilisation:
sick simian sentiment, sound human hate.
It is the seedy small-town railway station
where in the dust the dingy train we wait.
It is the bond between us, man and brother,
by which we hide our feelings from each other.

Long, long, after the last explosion,
when field and factory and public house
are gone, if spared the centuries' erosion,
our history will be a clockwork mouse.
A sleekit coorin' tim'rous beestie
become mechanical and nasty.

*

The solemn stars that frame the universe
and seem a settled order to the soul,
are only one-way motion of a hearse,
an empty juggernaut whose uncontrol
ranges a vacant meaningless immense,
posting to nowhere out of nothingness.

and in ourselves the never-ending search
of a sick actor for identity
another blank, a false proscenium arch
the front and focus of a malady:
a mirror-aspect of the same untruth—
but not the sickness! That is true enough.

Out of a devious denying world
to grasp at something solid is the need;
not beauty or the rest, since we are hurled
beauty and all, and fall with steady speed,
endlessly falling like poor Keats in Rome
endlessly dying in a little room.

Or else like Shelley on attenuate wire
mounting from strand to ever-thinning strand,
until at last, without it, even higher,
and the abandoned line comes down to hand.
Spiralling down, no menace to the birds,
so slight a thing it is, so purely words.

*

We die in drawing rooms we entertain,
bruising imagination on the bone,
or in a gentler, darker, limbo feign
lost things unlost, poor fragments deaf and dumb:
still-lifes of life recalled, dead anecdote,
the loving unresponsive voice remote.

This is a candle in a field at night
round which like moths such shadows flutter fast.
If the wind spares, the dew will quench its light,
it's not in nature its effect should last.
It is a song, sung in the wind and rain,
in a high wind when the tall trees complain.

And yet, recurrent: age to age expressed
in lines like these to catch a passing mood:
snares for delight, a loveliness at best
like light on waters, lost when most pursued.
Cobwebs on grasses in the morning sun,
lace for an hour or two and then undone.

King Claudius

Being so bad, how did he get to be king?
Being so wicked, how was he voted in?
Begin
with that.
That is the question.

Hamlet at thirty must have been well known.
So, what was wrong
other than he was seen to be unstable
compared to one so eminently able,
mad, or if less than mad,
then the more bad;
on any estimate far worse than Claudius,
Far more disastrous?

Consider, when you talk of murder
(to go no further)
Rosencranz, Guildenstern, sent to Hell—
for what? Because 'betwixt the fell
incensed points of mighty opposites'.
(Poor nits)
Gertrude, Ophelia, and Polonius!
It's Jack the Ripper as compared to Claudius.

Granted the latter's crime was fratricide—
though who are we to talk?—Besides,
he could have been a youth of promise too
whose expectation withered as it grew
under a strutting stuff-shirt till
he more than had his fill
of that feigned 'front of Jove' displayed to Heaven
as if anticipating television.
'Hyperion's curls!' (How vulgar could you get?
How tarted-up effeminate?)
Recall those 'sledded Polacks on the ice'.
Why so precise?
Where else would sledded Polacks be?

Easy to see
how Claudius, catching Gertrude's eye
in some such spate of blank blank verse verbosity,
saw love and murder meet.
And from that vision never could retreat.

What's certain is
that being so *un*majestical,
so little of a bore upon a pedestal,
not mad,
nor altogether bad,
King Claudius claims his due;
and recollect, of all that posturing crew,
he, only he, at close of day
retires to pray,
and for the first time speaking for himself
and his soul's health,
obliges you to feel
something of his appeal.

One thinks of Churchill on Lloyd George's death,
touching with moderated breath
that tortuous ascent
and then, abruptly and without exegesis—
'He *coveted* the place!
Perhaps the place was his.'

Mary Wollstonecraft

Reading of her, her sex's great front-runner,
the mixed-up ideology and feeling;
so right, so wrong, and yet so somehow true,
never in anything herself concealing ...

So brave, to be herself, self-contradicting.
Intelligent, but not too clever either.
Unworldly wise, I think best sums her up
as it might do of Noah about weather.

Wrong about everything, right in direction,
wrong for her time, but right for all of time,
assessing her across the centuries
it's easier to see the near-sublime,

to separate the dross of day to day
from that of spirit struggling to be free
from dear dependence as from servile shame
and see it spell responsibility.

Now, thinking of what followed her rough course—
illusionists like Byron, Godwin, Shelley.
How cardboard slight they seem compared to one
who loved them as mankind so bitter-bravely.

Samuel Dyer 1702—1749

'So modest, mellow, mild, and unassuming,
his temper so engaging, so controlled,
that even Johnson never interrrupted . . . '

Or hardly ever?

Sleekit, I think
and think that something—
perhaps the effect of television—
produces an aversion to mankind.
Continuing, I read that Edmund Burke
pronounced him much as has been quoted—
'Sincere, benevolent, profound.
The modesty and sweetness of his ways . . . ' etcetera.
His conversation said to be
'As amiable as instructive.'

A pouf! I half suspect
and note he was intended for the Church.
It makes no difference that he never made it.
Never, in fact, made anything.
The mild engaging youth became a man
mild and engaging, and in spite of erudition—
Greek, Latin, French, Italian—what you will,
and not forgetting mathematics—
'adopted no profession.' Which I take to mean
he did no work. It seems he simply lived,
and lived on dining out.

It may be there is something atavistic
in comment of this sort. Perhaps
I chide the Dyer in myself. I know
while watching pictures of the Palestine invasion
there was a cut-throat captive terrorist,
head blasted and the severed flesh
held by one hand above his blackened brows,
came hirpling on until he saw the set,

then stop to give the world a mock-salute,
a painful ruffian grin.
And how it was, I am at loss to say,
but all my Calvinistic heart went out to him.

Easter and After

He had seen them as ordinary men.
Some he had rather despised
until the hushed moment when
they appeared again to his eyes
'Utterly, utterly changed'
because of conviction and will,
from common affairs estranged
as though remote on a hill
they stood untopped alone,
MacDonagh and MacBride,
as if they were turned to stone
Connolly and Pearse beside;
and the small living things,
gulls adrift in the sky,
the moorhen's flurry of wings
at the horseman hurrying by,
were only the change and pass
of cloud and sun,
the rider a shadow on grass,
the men and the deed lived on.

They had 'turned their hearts to stone'.
It was 'sacrifice'.
The meaning for Heaven alone,
for us it should suffice
'to murmur name on name
as a mother . . . ' but why go on?
The words are words of fame
their spell too famously known.

By the grace of the BBC
and other similar graces
I have seen them on TV
the men with the insect faces.
Men so immeasurably dull
so far from heroic
too utterly, utterly null

to be even demonic.
Men of such coarse grained mind
as how should they speak
except by violence blind
for the thing they seek:
the song sung in the pub,
their name in a story,
a plaque in a working-man's club.
That kind of glory.

I come from a Scots border town,
undistinguished, small,
that at the Reformation
did something remarkable.
I mean it did nothing—no rout.
Papist and Protestant
took the kirk turnabout
to nobody's descant.
Nothing heroic yet great.
Even immense.
So far from sectarian hate
so much commonsense.

But 'Heaven' was the final recourse
of the dabbler in magic,
fascinated by force,
too small to be tragic.
A man with the gift of words
and limited vision,
a voice like the voice of birds
singing out of a prison.

MacDonagh and MacBride,
Connolly and Pearse,
he made them the reason they died
for the next to be worse.

Philip Larkin

He had a spider's solitariness.
Touchiness too. It showed in how he lived—
if 'lived' is what it was—
billeted on
a public life extraneousness
to him a prison.

So, he retreated, made excuses, failed
to answer letters, let it be understood
by whom it might concern
he was from home—
and that meant permanently. It was
his position.

But though maintained, desire to be apart
was not his universe. Always his thought
stretched out to what he shunned.
Oblivion
was forced to wait, and wait upon
his soft precision.

Now, to the crevice crack the body goes
to flake and moulder and be blown away,
the lineaments disappear,
the webs he spun
stir and respond to every living breath
love-tokens in the sun.

Ça Ira!

I see you posed, attache case in hand—
or better, reaching for it out of cars.
Ducking your head, an ostrich in the sand
yet instigator of my private wars.
I tell you everything for no comment—
unless it's in that crypto-case you carry:
some bomb, destructive of a mind's content
or an imagined loss, and I its quarry.
You tell me nothing; my performance falters
as we discourse—it's hardly more than that:
dead flowers dead men have laid on fading altars:
chit-chat.

So, case in hand, you come and go and leave me,
as if you were a blood-transfusion kit.
Blood, and a cup of tea, so you receive me,
not without terror either. Do you knit?
That's not at all extravagant. It's true!
You who think causes are worth violence.
I only think your eyes are violet-blue
and that, quite seriously, is better sense
whatever be their colour, for goodwill
transcends particulars. It is a flow
with nothing fatal in its overspill
and so

I stake against your certainties, my heart:
that politics are myths, you, self-deceived,
playing your worthy bloody-minded part,
when most in earnest least to be believed.
You do not like this: shuffle your worn pack
behind your brows, my insufficiency
betrays itself, encouraging attack
and sinks into a painful gaucherie,
where, while to scattered senses you appear
cobra-reflective, adamantinate,
I listen for the anger that I fear,
the hate.

Yet when you talk of Byron, Keats, and Shelley,
Wordsworth or Graves, Yeats, Eliot, Tennyson,
you catch their mood, evoke their spell—the
livingness, the pain, the loss, the benison.
You tell their story, but they tell you nothing
of *why* you tell. That's altogether lost
like a remembrance in old age of spring,
an arid, unfelt, intellectual ghost.
Well, understand, I have no truth to proffer
except myself, except myself and them,
not anything that politics can offer—
a poem.

How can you sink yourself in some pronouncement
of Ireland, Bangladesh, or Viet Nam,
as if your words did other than present
selective sympathy, and that a sham?
I know no way to cure the worlds's phobia,
no more, I think, do you, in spite of passion.
Tell me what happened to Estonia.
You don't remember? It's gone out of fashion.
Wrongs fade away when they are out of sight,
it's part of what's called making history.
You're with the big battalions when you fight,
not me.

Poetry's commitment of a different sort.
It takes no side, makes no comparison,
its essence is a matter of rapport,
its judgment is the universal sun.
It is perception naked to the truth
of beauty, and that other truth of cancer,
it is transcendent even to sick youth,
it is the light of joy, and that's no answer
except the joy is truth, truth poetry,
and poetry truth. Not quite as Keats has said it,
but as from out a desolate of pain, he
made it.

That I, an ageing man should see this clear—
or feel it, is the better way to put it—
is strange, but nothing half so queer
that you, with better brain, should so dispute it.
Yet the connection between thought and thought
and the event and thought you take as true,
moved in primeval slime, so we are taught,
and to conclusions much the same as you.
Since we are monsters raised it's not surprising
that monstrously we think we know what's right
for everybody else, though all our rising
was fight.

I see my life as part of a transition
to be got through, may be to live again.
It is a holding action, not a mission,
if mission, then to bear it, not ordain.
Better Andromeda abandoned, scared,
than be Prometheus to lead the blind—
the first of know-alls, naturally prepared
to bring down fire from Heaven upon mankind.
Andromeda in her predicament was
fully informed about the human level
and saw pro bono publico—that cant—as
evil.

Your own particular Utopia
may prove, like others, inappropriate,
no sweet post-slaughter cornucopia,
not great and good and just—just a police-state.
Plato, of course, put all the poets out.
The very first to go and with good reason.
They are the sort who ever raise the doubt.
Being of the breed himself he knew their treason.
My least dislike is for democracy,
not that I care about the common touch,
but muddle gives a chance to men like me.
Not much.

For poetry has few friends though many flatterers:
professional poet and professional Scot,
members of this and that and grant-aid scatterers,
the busy jobbers of the entrepôt.
I wish we had a Blackwoods and a Jeffrey.
They had their uses though one might despise:
reptiles get rid of lesser predatory,
acid's an antidote to funguses.
Slow, and reluctant to me comes the Muse.
She's without influence, as poor as birds.
I take the pay I cannot well refuse:
mere words.

The riddle of myself—my universe—
though of the strangest sort is no delusion
and still remains the subject of my verse
moving as if twofold to one conclusion:
I think we're God's dilemma. Given freewill,
what could he do but leave us to evolve it?
Spinning the top, and leave it spinning till
we use our fearful freedom to resolve it?
We are Gods's monsters whom he seeks to win
by love. What could he do to show it?
How else, but joy in pain could he begin—
poet?

Snow in Lent

For Judith

When I consider how my life is spent
and half of it unspent—not lived at all,
I am reminded of that snow in Lent
and how the heaviest and hoariest pall
lay on the sheltered cherry tree and on
the cloistered gable, but in thinnest white
the Cumbrian hills were etched bare to the bone
to make a prospect in the very heart of light;

and when this morning, reading your long letter
on Repton dig—those Anglo-Saxon graves
screening the Mesolithic shale and scatter
of flints and smearings, broken holes of staves,
the obliterate mask of ancient habitation,
rude shelters six, eight, thousand years ago
assembled to assume in meditation
dark images against an outline in the snow:

the starving fisher crouching in the reeds,
the furtive hunter lurking in the scree,
scene after scene approaches and recedes,
the leafless woods, the desolate estuary;
then from the miseries of the unnumbered dead
I draw a comfort unimaginable,
seeing the grave a universal bed
and that firm architecture underpinning all.

Last Words

Very strange those last recorded words.
    Goethe's 'More light!'
and other flickerings before
    The endless night.

Hardy at Max Gate in big brass bed
    waiting dismiss,
all stoic certainty—and then
    'What's this? What's this?'

No time to tell what he thought he saw,
    he promptly dies,
leaving astonishment behind
    at his surprise.

Or Henry Fifth of Agincourt
    ages ago
dwindling of dysentery, yelling
    'Not so! Not so!'

He had been pious in slaughter but,
    Christ receive us!
yammers on that his portion is with
    'the Lord Jesus!'

And Sterne propped up in four-poster
    at the last, slow.
Cowering, raising an arm to
    ward off a blow.

Terrible these, yet some have made jokes
    for final effect:
Voltaire, the bed curtains on fire,
    murmuring 'Not yet!'

But that sort of thing is uncommon.
    Most go like lambs—
except for my old uncle Peter
    reciting psalms

he had learned as a child, and I'm proud
    a relative
should pick such a good way to die—
    or even to live.

But not the best. Best was Anne Brontë
    brave girl who forgot
weakness, pain, even God and cried
    'Courage, Charlotte!'